W9-BYY-986

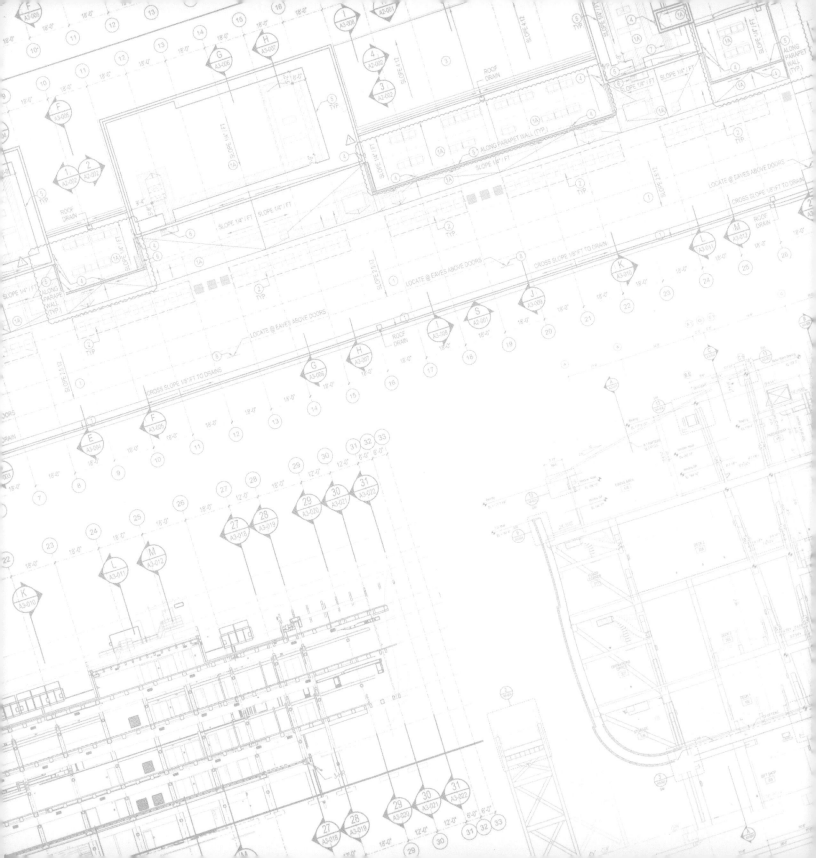

THE BUILDING OF THE
ARK ENCOUNTER

BY FAITH THE ARK WAS BUILT

Master Books®

First printing: August 2016
Fifth printing: August 2018

Master Books® is a division of the New Leaf Publishing Group, Inc.

ISBN: 978-0-89051-931-8
ISBN: 978-1-61458-546-6 (digital)
Library of Congress Number: 2016944939

Cover by Diana Bogardus
Cover photo by Peter Kappes

Unless otherwise noted, Scripture quotations are from the New King James Version®. Copyright © 1982 by Thomas Nelson. Used by permission. All rights reserved.

Please consider requesting that a copy of this volume be purchased by your local library system.

Printed in China

Please visit our website for other great titles:
www.masterbooks.com

For information regarding author interviews,
please contact the publicity department at (870) 438-5288.

Master Books®
A Division of New Leaf Publishing Group
www.masterbooks.com

The Vision — Ken Ham

Cost: Priceless

2004	2005	2006	2007	2008	2009	2010	2011	2012	2013	2014	2015	2016

Although my interest in Genesis and creation/evolution began when I was younger, my specific interest in the Flood and the Ark of Noah was intensified as a young adult in 1974. That's when I read *The Genesis Flood* by Morris and Whitcomb. I discovered that the global Flood was an integral event in regard to the topic of origins. That catastrophe explains most of the fossil record as well as the genetic bottleneck for humans and all the kinds of land-dependent, air-breathing animals. In fact, every person alive today is a descendent of Noah's sons, Shem, Ham, and Japheth, and so the Flood was certainly a major event in human history.

At times over the years people have asked me, "Wouldn't it be wonderful to find Noah's Ark?" Then people would suggest that it would be great to build Noah's Ark. So the idea of a reconstruction of the Ark has been bandied about for years in various discussions.

Then at some stage of the planning of a Creation Museum (in the early 2000s in the USA) and raising money for it, we began to talk about future projects. The subject of building an Ark came up again with the idea that it could be built across from the Creation Museum. We actually acquired a two-acre piece of property on the other side of the lake at the museum site. And then we purchased an additional 20 acres behind the Creation Museum that we thought would be suitable for building an Ark and for parking. However, a detailed national survey conducted by America's Research Group predicted that up to two million people a year would be visiting the Ark. So we looked elsewhere and eventually obtained 800 acres on Interstate 75 at exit 154 Williamstown, Kentucky, (south of Cincinnati) for the Ark Encounter project (about 40 miles from the museum).

At the Creation Museum, which opened in 2007, we have a spectacular Noah's Ark exhibit. It represents only one percent of the Ark's volume. The massive exhibit has become a very popular one for our museum visitors. A lot of people have commented about how much they liked that Ark exhibit; some have said that it is their favorite display at the museum. Many visitors have also commented how great it would be to experience the entire Ark structure.

In 2004, the leadership team at Answers in Genesis put together a strategic plan, with the help of an outside consultant. One of the items we listed in the plan as a future goal was to build a life-size Noah's Ark. This plan was presented to the AiG board in 2005, and that year, the board agreed to make the Ark the number one priority after the Creation Museum was opened.

Building a Team

When we were in the early stages of building the Creation Museum, a man living in Japan, Patrick Marsh, reached out to us. He explained that he had worked for the Universal Studios theme park and other attractions around the world. He was a Christian and biblical creationist who wanted to use his talents for the Lord in designing exhibits for the future Creation Museum. We hired him, and Patrick brought another level of expertise and professionalism to the design and construction of the exhibits—ideas that we never envisioned. He took the script I had written for the teachings we wanted to present in the museum, and Patrick and a talented design team he assembled turned the script into the phenomenal world-class museum that we see today. Even many evolutionists who have toured the museum have stated that the Creation Museum is the best-looking, most high-tech museum they have seen. When the secular media ask me how we were able to assemble such a talented, qualified design team, my standard response has been: "Just as God brought the land animals to Noah for the Ark, so God brought these people to us." There's no doubt that it was only the hand of God that could have put together the entire gifted staff, and others outside the ministry, to make the Creation

Museum, and soon the Ark Encounter, what we see today.

People often ask me if the Creation Museum turned out to be what I first envisioned. The answer: "absolutely not!" Yes, certainly the message of the 7 C's of history and having a walk through history were a part of the original vision for the museum. But God brought Patrick (and the others in his team) to take the exhibits and the impact to a whole new level, beyond anything we could ever have imagined. Patrick has a very special place in this ministry. And even though he is a very humble guy, Patrick, and those alongside him, took the Creation Museum to a level that is better than what a visitor will experience in just about any museum or themed attraction in the secular world.

Because of all that expertise the Lord brought to us, plus a broad base of donors, the AiG board had the confidence to move ahead and start building the Ark. Just as with the

Creation Museum, the Ark project has greatly exceeded what we originally envisioned. With the Lord's blessing, the Ark-themed attraction has been taken to a whole new level of quality and impact—for the purpose of evangelism in this very secularized culture.

Bigger and Better

One of my father's favorite verses of Scripture was "And whatever you do, do it heartily, as to the Lord and not to men" (Colossians 3:23). Yes, we want to honor the Lord in all we do. And because we have the greatest and most important message in the universe to proclaim, the gospel, AiG believed that what we should build must be as good as, or better than, what the secular world does. Just like with the Creation Museum, we wanted to make the Ark project as good as what Hollywood can do. We also wanted to use the marketing methods that the secular world uses, such as TV commercials, blockbuster trailers, billboards, and more. We wanted to go into the world and encourage people to

come and experience the message of God's Word and the gospel that the world so desperately needs. God, through His miraculous hand, brought the expertise to us so that we could build another world-renowned attraction—a biblically themed attraction—that would glorify Him, and bring honor to Him and His Word in every way.

The best way to describe the life-size Ark, part of an entire theme park we call Ark Encounter, is that it consists of exhibits, within an exhibit, within an exhibit. You see, the massive Ark itself is an exhibit, and the inside of this wooden structure is an exhibit as well. And the 132 Ark bays on the three decks contain stunning teaching exhibits.

Why do I say that the life-size Ark is an exhibit in itself? Most people, for the very first time, will begin to understand the immense size of this ship Noah built when they first approach the Ark. Then as I've taken people inside the Ark, a true timber-framed structure being the biggest of its kind in the world, it is a jaw-dropping

Ken and Mally with their five children and 14 grandchildren.

experience for them. They will say something like, "This is amazing. Simply amazing." There's just something about all the timber inside. Of course, God created wood, and there is something about it, especially with the enormous amount of wood seen inside the Ark, that absolutely fascinates people. They love the look and feel of it. Guests often stop and contemplate the massive beams and the craftsmanship that went into the building of the Ark structure. They also notice the complexity of the Ark's engineering and architecture. This gives us an opportunity to help them think about Noah and his brilliance in the correct way. You see, many people (even unwittingly) have adopted an evolutionary view of history, thinking that ancient people were less intelligent and less advanced than we are today. People have often asked me "How could Noah have built such a ship?" But, from a creationist perspective, ancient people would have been highly intelligent.

Ancient Artistry

Within the great ship, the startling exhibits showcase the extraordinary talent of our outstanding team of designers, fabricators, sculptors, artisans, and others. The exhibits go into detail about such things as: what Noah's family might have experienced on the Ark; answer questions about how Noah could fit the animals on board and then feed and look after them; offer teaching exhibits about trusting God's Word; present the gospel in our secularized age; display various cages, artifacts, life-size figures, and unique sculpted animals; show the sensational artwork; present teaching exhibits about the Flood and Ark; and the list goes on.

But what's the real purpose of the Ark? I say that other than the Cross, the Ark is the greatest reminder of the message of salvation. Noah had to place one door in the Ark—and only those who went through that one door were saved from the watery judgment. God's Son stepped into history to become Jesus Christ, the God-Man. Just as Noah and his family went through the Ark's only

door to be saved, so too do we need to go through the one "door." Jesus said, "I am the door. If anyone enters by Me, he will be saved, and will go in and out and find pasture" (John 10:9). He also declared: "I am the way, the truth, and the life. No one comes to the Father except through Me" (John 14:6).

As we look at the decline of our Western culture today, Christians will notice many similarities to the wicked days of Noah. Genesis 6:5 records: "Then the Lord saw that the wickedness of man was great in the earth, and that every intent of the thoughts of his heart was only evil continually." What a time it is today to build an Ark to remind people that God is a righteous God who judges wickedness. But just as God provided salvation to Noah and his family, God has provided an Ark of salvation for us today: through Christ's death on the Cross and His Resurrection. Each of us needs to go through the "door," the Lord Jesus Christ, to be in the Ark of salvation.

After Jesus was crucified, there was a big stone, like a door, that was rolled over the tomb. That door was opened when Jesus rose from the dead. In the Ark, there will be exhibits that deal with the various doors in Scripture. And as we teach about those doors, we will be challenging visitors as to where they are concerning Christ's free gift of salvation!

Yes, the Ark Encounter is an evangelistic Ark. It will be one of the greatest Christian outreaches of our era. It's all a part of making sure we "do business until" He comes (Luke 19:13). We're to be doing the business of the King, proclaiming the truth of God's Word and the gospel.

As you visit the Ark Encounter and gaze at what some are calling a new wonder of the modern world, I urge you to ponder Genesis 6:22: "Thus Noah did; according to all that God commanded him, so he did."

No wonder Noah is listed in what's often called the "Believers Hall of Fame" in Hebrews 11! May we be bold people of faith, just like Noah!

The Plan — LeRoy S. Troyer, FAIA

Cost: $4,000,000

2004	2005	2006	2007	2008	2009	2010	2011	2012	2013	2014	2015	2016

It has been a dream of mine to build something of this size out of wood that honors and glorifies our Lord. As I look back, it seems my whole life has been preparing me for this adventure and what an adventure it has been. This master plan for the Ark Encounter is the largest and boldest project we (The Troyer Group) have ever undertaken in the history of the firm.

My parents were Amish, so I was raised in an Amish community near Middlebury, Indiana, on a farm. As I reflect back on my life, it seems God was preparing me for something as a young boy working on a farm. We had 30 acres of woods from which we harvested trees and sawed them by hand. I would help build barns (frolics) with the Amish community, so I was around large-frame wooden structures at a very young age. Later on, we got a chainsaw, but very few people had such an item when I was growing up. I enjoyed working with wood back then, and I still do.

One day my fourth grade teacher, Ms. Miller, introduced various professions to the class, and architecture was one I thought I'd like to do. When I was 16 I started to learn drafting by copying architectural drawings. During the day, I'd help build buildings, and at night, I would do drawings for the contractor—that's how I learned. I built my own T-square and drawing board, and I traced drawings by the light of an old kerosene lamp at age 16 or 17. Then I started doing drawings for a local contractor. I didn't get paid for the drawing work for three years. I did this just to learn, considering the work part of a low-cost education.

At age 14, after I recovered from polio, I told my parents that I did not want to stay in the Amish faith and instead wanted to join the Mennonite church. They blessed that decision, so I have been associated with the Mennonite faith since that time. When I was 21, and married, an architecture firm in South Bend, Indiana, heard about me and offered me a job as a draftsman. I worked with this firm for quite some time. In 1965, I was accepted into Notre Dame's architecture program, even without a high school education. It was a five-year program, and this was an exciting time in my life. My wife Phyllis and I took our three sons to study in Rome, Italy, for a year and traveled to many countries in Europe to study architecture. After graduation in 1971, I passed the national boards, so I was now a board-certified architect with a degree from Notre Dame. I started the Troyer Group the same year, and here we are. Today, we employ around 40 people and have built churches, universities, retirement communities, destinations, and family attractions, and many other projects all over the United States as well as work in different countries.

Realizing the Possibility

However, there is one project that we helped design that was very special, the American Country Farmers Market, the largest wood-pegged barn in the country located in Elkhart, Indiana. This is an all-wood structure that has some huge timber in it. What is interesting is its cupolas are close to the height of the main structure of the Ark, and although the building is not as wide as the Ark, it is about two thirds as long. Orie and Ernest Lehman and David and his son Rudy Bontrager worked on the project in Elkhart. I grew up with them because they were in the Amish community. I stayed in touch with them, and they did buildings like the Farmers Market and others in the Middlebury and Shipshewana, Indiana, area. So, once again this was another learning process in preparing me for the future Ark project.

Then about 25 years ago, an elderly Mennonite businessman from Pennsylvania approached me and said, "LeRoy, could you design an ark in Florida? I have an idea of building a Noah's Ark on an Interstate cloverleaf in Florida. It will have lodging and a restaurant, and I'd like to furnish each room with a different animal theme." So I did a few sketches of his idea and drew up some rough plans. I knew some of his adult children, and as I talked to them and they told me they didn't think he had enough money for the project, I discouraged him from moving forward. But I had already put some time into thinking about an Ark. From a Kingdom perspective, I thought the Ark project was something I could get my arms around as a mission because of what it can do as an educational tool for all people, and as a witness for non-Christians to come and see "by faith Noah built the Ark, by faith Abraham... by faith Jacob... by faith Joseph...."

The size of the Ark is enormous. The Bible tells us the length of Noah's Ark was 300 cubits, its width 50 cubits, and its height 30 cubits. A cubit is an ancient measurement of length based on the distance from the elbow to the tip of the longest finger. The actual length of a cubit varied between different ancient groups of people.

LeRoy Troyer and Mike Zovath signing contracts in January of 2013.

LeRoy Troyer, owner and founder of the Troyer Group, outside the construction trailer on the Ark site.

In large-scale construction projects, ancient civilizations typically used the long cubit (about 19.8–20.6 in [52 cm]). Here at the Ark Encounter, we've chosen to use the Hebrew long cubit. At 20.4 inches, this makes the Ark about 510 feet long, over 50 feet tall, and 85 feet wide. So we are having to design and oversee and manage the construction of what will be the largest heavy timber-framed structure in the world of this type of building.

I remember taking Ken Ham and some of the board members of Answers in Genesis to the farmers market building in Elkhart six or seven years ago. When they saw the building, the large timbers and the scale of it, they were encouraged because after looking at the structure they really thought the Ark could be built today at the appropriate size with similar techniques as ancient shipbuilders. I believe it also gave them confidence in me and the Troyer group.

Design — Just the Beginning

Building an Ark in the 21st century is much different than what Noah had to do. We have codes, state laws, permits, safety and liability issues, and being mostly wood, it has

a number of challenges from a design standpoint. Then on top of that, building a structure out of wood this large means you have fire ratings, wind loads, and more that must also be considered. This meant we needed to find wood that had a strong fiber strength. Every species of wood has different fiber strength so we needed wood that could take the required stress, and both the Engelmann Spruce and Douglas Fir are just such a wood.

The timber is carrying a heavy load and also a lot of wind pressures. We wanted to design the structure 10 to 15 percent over the code for wind pressure, so it can now handle over 120 mph winds. The concrete masonry towers are key to supporting and handling the wind load. That was one of the main reasons for the towers, to help anchor the Ark and to house the four large exit stairs, elevators, and restrooms.

We set the Ark on a structural concrete platform, 15 feet above the ground since we didn't want the earth contacting the wood directly. That's one reason for the concrete platform which also allowed the project to have a large future restaurant on the roof of the Ark to accommodate 750 people at one time. It also helps to

An overview of the property along Interstate 75 between Cincinnati, Ohio, and Lexington, Kentucky, at the Williamstown, Kentucky, exit. The property covers 800 acres, and is about 40 minutes south of Cincinnati. The star is the general location of the Ark.

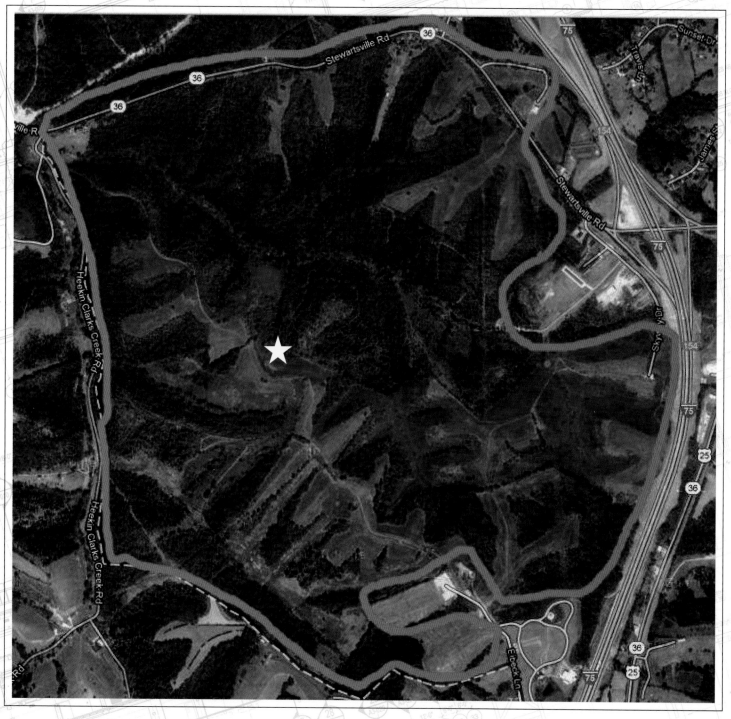

set the scale of the Ark having it sitting up off the ground some 15 feet, so I love how the platform presents the sheer size of the Ark. The Ark also has exits that can accommodate 10,000 guests at one time, along with 132 exhibit bays designed and built for guests to see and enjoy, including ancient Bible manuscripts.

Thousands of man-hours went into the design of this project. We probably have four to five thousand sheets of drawings which detail every aspect of the Ark. My role as president of The Troyer Group and architect is overseeing every stage of the project.

My life has been spent organizing and engaging other people, and so the key to me to build this Ark was to try to get the best people we could find, either in-house or outside of our office. We had at least 10 construction crews involved in the framing process. How do you get those crews to work together in harmony? The key is to engage people and do team building long before construction starts. I say it has been successful. Together we built it. We've had a few minor tension points. We've tried to get the guys to buy into the mission of the project and that has been very helpful in building the team atmosphere.

There are very few people in the world who know how to work with large heavy timber like this. There are 3.3 million board-feet of wood in the Ark that must be put together. I knew the skills of the Amish builders because of working with them in the past. So I asked them to head up the heavy timber framing and carpentry work. I also knew they had good people skills, and that was really key. That's why I said at the beginning, "having the right people at the right place, at the right time." It's really about people, and they are creative craftsman. None of us have all the answers, but together we can figure things out. I learned from being in construction at an early age that it's not the architect, engineers, and contractor who

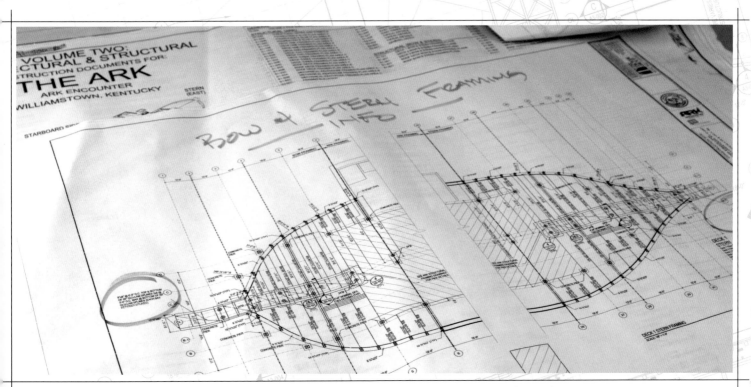

The plans for the bow and stern were very complicated, taking a great amount of teamwork to design.

The long awaited permit is finally in the hands of Mike Zovath, Ken Ham, and Patrick Marsh.

The Answers in Genesis board members bow for a time of prayer at the Ark property prior to the beginning of construction.

ARK SUPERIMPOSED ON CONCRETE PYLONS

LeRoy and Ken at the viewing platform just days before the first bent was lifted into place.

know everything. It's a team effort, and that's been my philosophy.

Another key to all this was the structural design team put together by The Troyer Group and an engineering firm in Idaho that helped with the bow and stern. Colorado Timber Frame in Lafayette, Colorado, did the milling and hatching for the heavy timbers. They milled all the timber and large logs to the design and specs given. There is also an Amish metal fabricating shop, JOMAR, located in Middlebury, Indiana, that fabricated approximately 4,000 steel connections, weighing over 142,000 lbs. It would have been difficult to deal with another steel fabricating

company, as JOMAR has had experience working with wood and has been great to work with.

Then all the parts came together in Williamstown, Kentucky, on I-75 at exit 154. The heavy timbers, some logs over four feet in diameter, were assembled on site. Half of a framing section (or bent), weighing 35,000 pounds, was lifted in place by a large crane. We had very few problems as all the firms and craftsmen did a great job working together with the complex design. Considering nothing like this has been built in the recent past, we consider this truly an engineering marvel.

From this drawing, one can see some of the detail in the bow and stern, as well as the different decks. There are also ramps throughout the Ark structure to make it very handicap friendly.

A cubit is an ancient measurement of length based on the distance from the elbow to the tip of the longest finger. The actual length of a cubit varied between different ancient groups of people. Here are some samples: Hebrew short: 15.5" – Egyptian: 17.6" – Common 18" – Babylonian royal: 19.8" – Egyptian Royal: 20.6" – and the Hebrew long 20.4".

The Ark Encounter used the Hebrew long cubit. The Bible tells us the length of Noah's Ark was 300 cubits, its width 50 cubits, and its height 30 cubits. So the Ark was over 510' long, 50' high and over 85' wide.

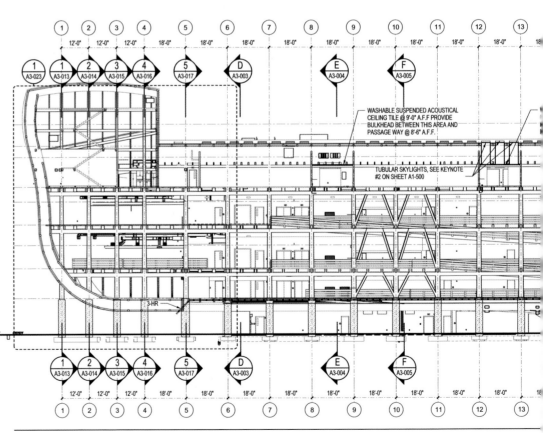

A Race to the Finish

The large round sloping logs, some 32–36" in diameter, as well as the bow and the stern have been the most difficult and challenging parts of the actual construction of the Ark. The complexity of this challenge was almost overwhelming, but by working together as a team, we did it. We were pushed for time and had to use an outside engineering firm to help us finish the structural plans for the bow and stern. And to keep the project on the tight timeframe that we had, we needed to get the plans to Colorado Timber Frame so they could start cutting the timber. It was the same with all the steel connections that would be needed. First order of business was team

building, and then the team designed and built a replica of Noah's Ark for everyone to see and experience.

The Ark is the first phase of an 800-acre Ark Encounter biblically themed attraction for people of all ages to visit and learn about the Bible's historical accounts, such as how God saved humanity and that He wants us today to honor and glorify Him. It is by faith that Noah built the Ark!

Drawing by Troyer Group

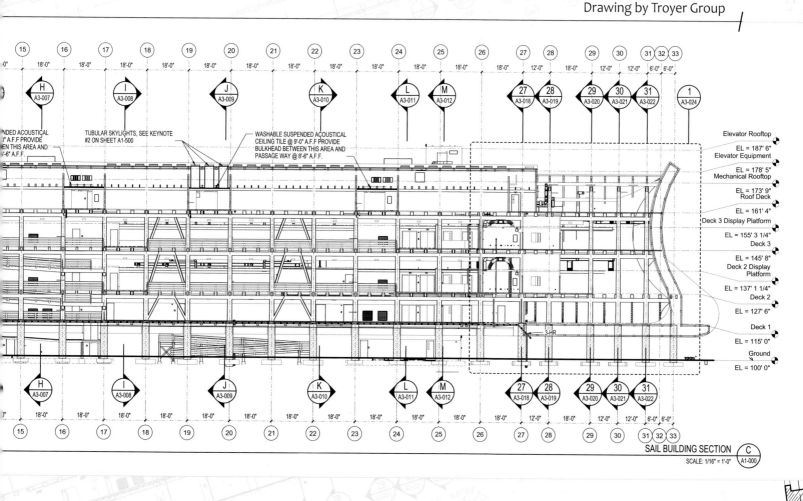

SAIL BUILDING SECTION
SCALE: 1/16" = 1'-0"

Moving Dirt

Cost: $3,000,000 Ark Site
Cost: $6,000,000 Parking Lot

	2014																	2016				
Aug.	Sept.	Oct.	Nov.	Dec.	Jan.	Feb.	Mar.	Apr.	May	Jun.	Jul.	Aug.	Sept.	Oct.	Nov.	Dec.	Jan.	Feb.	Mar.	Apr.	May	Jun.

Excavation begins on the Ark site August 2014.

The view at the end of the first day of excavation.

Large Caterpillar scrapers like this one can haul up to 50 yards of dirt at a time.

The progress after one month of excavation.

One of the many large trucks that can haul up to 100 tons of dirt and rock.

A glimpse of the property in the spring of 2014, before excavation began. The Ark site is below and the parking lot on the opposite page.

After 5 months of work, the site was finally ready for the construction to begin on the Ark, having moved over 500,000 yards of dirt and hauling in hundreds of loads of gravel to a thickness of 12". Ken Ham stands to the right with his arms outstretched showing where the Ark will go, and to the left is a foundation for one of the towers.

A model of the parking lot showing how it has been designed to handle heavy traffic flow.

The location of the parking lot that will hold over 4,000 cars. One million yards of dirt were moved and rearranged to level off this lot. Buses will haul visitors one mile from the parking lot to the Ark site, giving them their first full glimpse of this amazing representation of God's grace.

Foundation, Piers & Slab

Cost: $3,000,000

2014					2015											2016					
Aug.	Sept.	Oct.	Nov.	Dec.	Jan.	Feb.	Mar.	Apr.	May	Jun.	Jul.	Aug.	Sept.	Oct.	Nov.	Dec.	Jan.	Feb.	Mar.	Apr.	May	Jun.

The very first foundation dug on the site.

Concrete being poured into a footing.

A few of the footings after they had been poured.

The rebar cages being placed and wired into the footings.

A 50,000-gallon holding tank (cistern) for extra fire protection throughout the wooden Ark structure.

Ken Ham standing next to
one of the large piers.

Pre-stressed concrete slabs were laid on top of
the piers to make a bed for the Ark.

These piers are 12½ feet tall, and there are 102 such piers from the bow to the stern of the Ark.

It was determined early on that the Ark would sit up off the ground and be built on piers for several reasons. One, you have an enormous amount of weight, so a solid and secure foundation was required. The overall weight of the Ark is 31,200,000 lbs. or 15,600 tons, so these piers and foundations were designed to take a load! Two, it was vital that the Ark be made out of wood, so it would have to be up off the ground. This allows one to come up under the Ark with queue lines, entrances to the Ark, etc., without affecting the overall look of the Ark.

With this overhead view, one can see the pillars and precast slabs being put into place. The towers are beginning to rise as well.

Once the pre-cast slabs were placed, the seams were filled with concrete and a layer of concrete was poured over the top. This helped smooth everything up, and strengthened the bed the Ark would rest upon. The opening in the middle is for the ramp that will come up from the ground level into the first floor of the Ark, and how visitors will exit.

The foundations, piers, and concrete bed all completed, ready to start receiving the first bents. Under the supervision of the Amish, team leaders begin their construction on the ground, with the first lift just a few days away.

Orie and Ernest Lehman (brothers) oversee the heavy timber construction.

Towers

Cost $3,200,000

2014					2015												2016					
Aug.	Sept.	Oct.	Nov.	Dec.	Jan.	Feb.	Mar.	Apr.	May	Jun.	Jul.	Aug.	Sept.	Oct.	Nov.	Dec.	Jan.	Feb.	Mar.	Apr.	May	Jun.

Block-laying began in early February during a strong cold front. For days the high temperatures did not rise above freezing, so a tent was built and heat pumped in so work could begin. The blocklayers were very dedicated to this project, which took close to a year to complete.

At the six-foot mark on the first tower.

Making good progress on the towers.

The towers beginning to go up, around 20-feet high.

The rebar that went into much of the block for extra strength.

The block crew working high up on the scaffolding.

The scaffolding at a height of 60 feet.

In March of 2015, those at the site were greeted with a beautiful rainbow late in the afternoon.

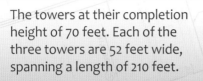

The towers at their completion height of 70 feet. Each of the three towers are 52 feet wide, spanning a length of 210 feet.

The utilities, heating and cooling, restrooms, elevators, and electrical grid are all in the towers, shown in images on the left. There are stairs in all three towers that will be used for emergency purposes only. With the added stairs in case of an emergency, the Ark can exit 10,000 people in six to eight minutes. With all the utilities in the towers, the authentic look of the Ark can be maintained.

The towers were built and attached in such a way as to handle winds of more than 120 miles per hour, which exceeds the code requirements. These are massive structures that really anchor the Ark, so to speak, in several ways.

This picture shows the initial construction as well as the outline of what will be the rest of the Ark when completed; notice the proximity and position to the towers.

Timber Preparation

Cost: $6,750,000

2014					2015											2016					
Aug.	Sept.	Oct.	Nov.	Dec.	Jan.	Feb.	Mar.	Apr.	May	Jun.	Jul.	Aug.	Sept.	Oct.	Nov.	Dec.	Jan.	Feb.	Mar.	Apr.	May	Jun.

Dan Manthei, (AiG board member) standing in a lane of thousands of board feet of raw timber ready for the Ark project.

Colorado **Timberframe**

The very first beam sized and fitted for the Ark project, February 25, 2015.

More timber awaiting the team at Colorado Timberframe to size and fit for the Ark.

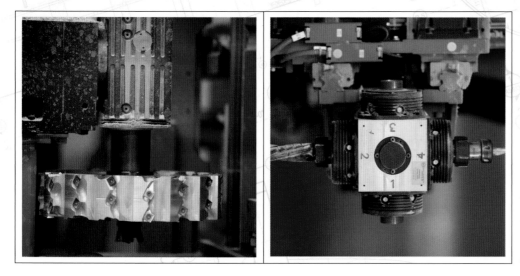

The larger top mill head can cut most joinery such as half laps, tenons, and bird-mouth connections. The small black mill underneath is called a dovetail mill, which cuts male and female dovetail joinery (far left).

The turret mill, better known as the revolver mill, can be rotated 360 degrees and can hold up to four tools (left).

T his revolutionary handling system has two gripper and guide wagons guaranteeing maximum precision during processing, even with warped and twisted beams (right).

Colorado Timberframe used CNC (Computer Numerical Control) technology. This equipment was recently upgraded so that it would be able to perform and do the largest size timber of any company in North America. This CNC machine can do anything needed with these timbers including mortise and tenon joints, drilling holes, and making notches for the steel plates that the timber will need at the Ark site (Bottom left and below).

Building the Ark Encounter created a fascinating combination of the latest technology, paired with ancient knowledge of woodworking and ship design.

These logs are Engelmann Spruce that were harvested out of a forest in Utah. They were responsibly harvested because they were already dead trees that were just taken out of the forest before they rotted. Now, they are being repurposed and put into a structure like the Ark so that everybody who goes through it can enjoy the character, size, and magnitude of these logs. They are unbelievable logs; some are over 50 inches in diameter.

Below is the log template built to fabricate the round logs. It needed a consistent jig, able to rotate the log and to do the necessary joinery. Every one of these logs has to be cut by hand. It takes six men two days to cut just one log, so it is an incredible amount of work. Large scale projects like this one are complicated. The complexity of the connections and how the timbers connect into one another is mind boggling. This is going to be the largest timber frame structure in the entire world. It's an engineering feat.

A good example of the many holes
that had to be precision drilled by
the CNC machine.

Labeling was a big part of the process so each customized
piece could be placed in the correct bay of the Ark.

Above you can see the finished logs that have been notched and drilled, being prepared for shipping.

Here you can see the scale of this log. There are 20 adults standing on it and they still look small. Keenan Tompkins, the owner of Colorado Timberframe, is standing in the center.

One of 88 truckloads heading to the Ark site.

The last shipment of timber being sent to the Ark. The first timber was cut on February 2015, and this last load shipped out in March 2016.

| Here are the ribs as the glue is applied. | The laminating crew works to bend the ribs to the proper shape by putting the beam into metal forms. This is a process that must be done both accurately and swiftly. The ribs are kept in these forms until the beam sets. |

The ribs have been taken out of the metal forms and planed on the wide surface.

The fabrication department
works diligently to cut the beams
to the proper shape. Notice the
plywood template on the floor.
The pattern makers designed this
actual size template in order to
ensure complete accuracy.

Timber Construction

Cost: $6,000,000

2014					**2015**														**2016**			
Aug.	Sept.	Oct.	Nov.	Dec.	Jan.	Feb.	Mar.	Apr.	May	Jun.	Jul.	Aug.	Sept.	Oct.	Nov.	Dec.	Jan.	Feb.	Mar.	Apr.	May	Jun.

One of the many 48-foot long Engelmann Spruce logs being off-loaded at the site. These logs traveled 1,200 miles from Lafayette, Colorado, to Williamstown, Kentucky. They hauled four at a time, so it took 16 truckloads to bring in the 64 logs needed for the project.

One can see the notches in the log where it will be assembled into a bent.

Each log is numbered, with bent information showing exactly where it will go.

A pile of the cross beams that connect the bents together.

Laminated ribs ready to be assembled with heavy timber.

The process of putting together the first bent began. The cranes were placing the timbers on cribs to help get them all level. Under the direction of the Amish team, the largest timber frame project in the world began.

Putting together the first bent took a lot of planning. The team painted the ground with a grid to help with the process. There are 15 massive timbers, logs, and beams that have to be put together for each half bent.

The Answers in Genesis board with their spouses and some of the leaders from the Troyer Group stand in front of the first bent as it is being put together.

The bents were divided into two halves, indicated on plans with an A, B, C, and D. The A and B bents are on the front side (port) of the Ark, and the C and D bents are on the back side (starboard). The first bent is put together, ready to be lifted into place.

On June 15, 2015, the first bent was lifted into place. There was a great deal of concern about the weight of the bent (25,000 pounds) and the stress this would put on all of the connections. It took two cranes to pick it up and get it vertical, then "Big Red" to move it into place.

All three timbers must fit perfectly into three steel plates, with a variance of only about 1/16 of an inch, or the bolts will not go through.

"Big Red" is capable of lifting 235 tons at a time. With incredible precision, it slips "bent 18 — grid C" into the steel sleeve.

An aerial view of the bent as it was put in place. This image shows just half the bent, and one can see between it and the crane where the other half bent will go.

Here one can see the progress being made as the Amish team puts together more bents. The first one took two weeks to assemble and raise into place. They were eventually able to do two in a week's time.

An overhead view with the first two bents in place and some of the crossbeams in place securing it all together, along with some large beams for bracing.

The Ark construction with six bents fully in place.

This photo shows 15 bents in place, and starting on the outer skin as well.

49

Most of the logs are over 4 feet in diameter.

Tim Dudley and Ken Ham show the size of these massive logs.

The Engelmann Spruce logs are simply beautiful, towering some 70 feet within the Ark. They were dead standing in the forests of Utah after a fire some years earlier, so they were responsibly harvested, and perhaps they are so awe-inspiring because they are one of God's creations.

On the first deck one can see the long line of impressive timber support throughout this large structure.

All the beams and supports connected together, showing the framework
of what is now the largest timber-framed building in the world.

Here one can see the three floors of the Ark, starting with the cement of deck one, then decks two and three.

To the left, the heavy timber framing shown here is Douglas fir coming from Oregon and Washington. Ranging in size from 20 inches by 20 inches by 32 feet, to the floor joists which are 16 inches by 18 inches by 14 feet.

Above, the decking is starting to go down over the floor joists. There will be a total of 600,000 board-feet of this decking put down. Over 290,000 board-feet of bamboo flooring will be laid over the decking.

The outer skin or siding was all built on the ground. It started with the laminated beams that were part of the bents. These were all the same size and used to fill in between the bents.

The team built a platform from which they would work on the sections. They then tied the laminated beams together with 2 x 4's, adding a plywood decking over it. They also added a moisture protection wrap.

The crane lifts this section into place, as the men bolt it down. One down, 31 more to go.

The construction crew applying the Radiata pine to the Ark. The finished product looks fantastic.

You can get an idea of the scale of the Ark when you look at the people toward the top of the picture.

Here the outside planks are being applied to the Ark. The planks are made of Radiata pine that is turned into Accoya®, a treated wood created via the acetylation wood modification process, using acetic anhydride (vinegar).

Accoya® wood is manufactured via a non-toxic treatment and uses fast-growing softwood timber from sustainable sources. The treated wood has very high durability and dimensional stability, allowing for reduced maintenance. This planking is guaranteed for 50 years. The Radiata pine is harvested in New Zealand, shipped to the Netherlands for the acetylation process, transported to North Carolina for milling, and then shipped to the site for installation.

Stern

The stern (back of the Ark) was the first end of the Ark to be built. Each bent is a little smaller in width as they start to curve in. Building this out of wood is quite complex, as wood does not just turn on its own; it has to be designed and engineered just right. There are hundreds of timbers that had to be cut, and every one was a different size. Thousands of holes had to be pre-drilled to exact specifications. Recreating the Ark has only been done a few times in history, since Noah's day, and took several thousand man hours to design. You can also see the large "stern projection" sticking out and going up to the roof deck. This was thought to make the Ark more stable in the rough seas after the Flood. The stern reaches a height of close to 80 feet.

Bow

The bow or "sail" on the Ark is a rigid wooden structure rather than a traditional sail that can be moved for propulsion purposes. Rather than calling it a "sail," it would be more accurate to call it a stem-post projection or a bow fin.

A bow fin would have served as an obstruction to the wind, pushing the bow away from the wind and the waves, preventing the Ark from capsizing. In tandem with the bow fin, a "stern projection" would have reduced the swaying of the Ark's stern, thus preventing it from being pushed side-on by the wind. So these additional structures on the top of the Ark were designed to provide stability. When completed, the bow will reach 104 feet off the ground.

Inside the Ark

Cost: $10,000,000

2014					2015								2016										
Aug.	Sept.	Oct.	Nov.	Dec.	Jan.	Feb.	Mar.	Apr.	May	Jun.	Jul.	Aug.	Sept.	Oct.	Nov.	Dec.	Jan.	Feb.	Mar.	Apr.	May	Jun.	

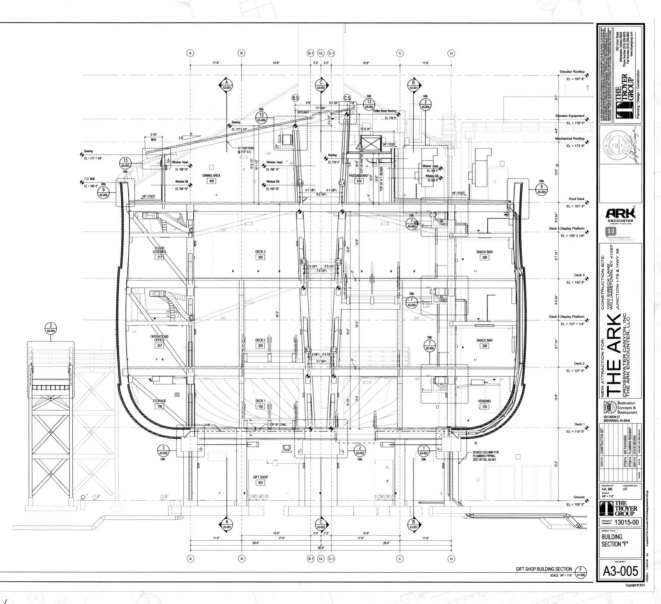

To the left, plans show how the inside of the Ark and its floors are laid out.

Visible here are decks 1, 2, & 3 and the roof deck. In the picture below the roof deck construction had not begun.

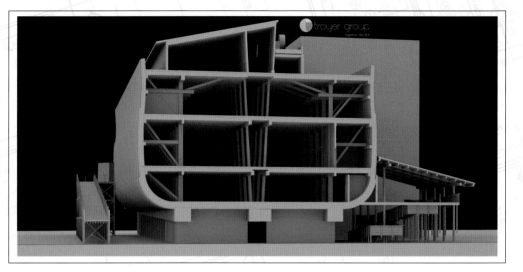

Below is a view of the stern from the bottom deck (level 1). You can see the many ribs coming together to point towards the stern. The massive logs and timbers are on display here in this beautiful panorama.

To the right, one can see the grid on the inside of the Ark. When all of the bents are tied together with the heavy timber, they make the frame of the floor. The covered bundles hold the flooring that will go down next. The tongue and groove flooring is 6 inches thick and designed to handle the 5- to 6-foot spans.

On the right are the large ramps that will take people up through the different floors very gradually. There are no stairways in the Ark, so it is very wheelchair accessible.

Below is another cutaway showing the ramps that will take people through the Ark.

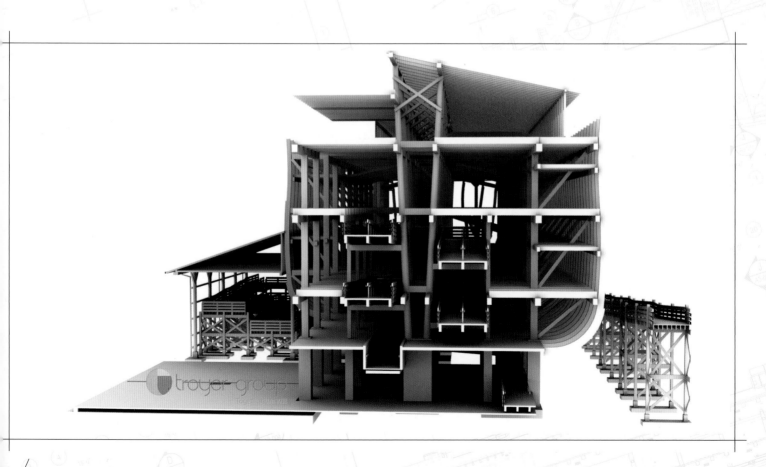

Looking down a long hallway, one can see the many exhibit bays on the right.

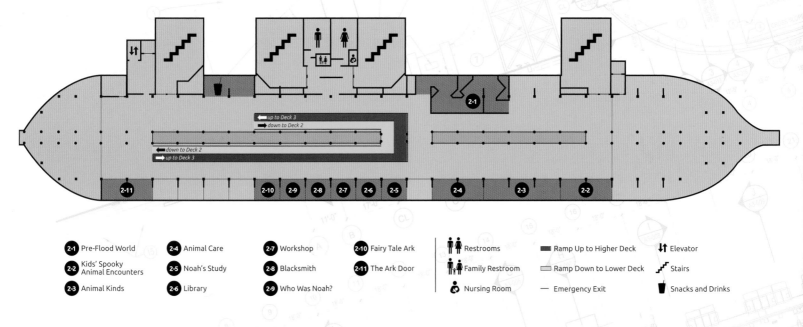

up to Deck 3
down to Deck 2

down to Deck 2
up to Deck 3

2-11   2-10 2-9 2-8 2-7 2-6 2-5   2-4   2-3   2-2

2-1	Pre-Flood World	2-4	Animal Care	2-7	Workshop	2-10	Fairy Tale Ark		Restrooms		Ramp Up to Higher Deck		Elevator
2-2	Kids' Spooky Animal Encounters	2-5	Noah's Study	2-8	Blacksmith	2-11	The Ark Door		Family Restroom		Ramp Down to Lower Deck		Stairs
2-3	Animal Kinds	2-6	Library	2-9	Who Was Noah?				Nursing Room	—	Emergency Exit		Snacks and Drinks

Deck 2 Exhibit Layout

Installation of exhibits is underway in the garden area, bird cages, and Noah's workshop.

Beginning to lay the bamboo flooring that will go throughout the entire structure.

Ararat Ridge Zoo

Ziplines

1,500 Seat
Restaurant

Guest Services

An overview of the entire project, from the actual Ark in the center left, to the parking lot on the far right. This picture was taken 60 days before opening.

Tram Road

Ticket Booth

4,000 Car Parking Lot

Freeway

Building of the Exhibits — **Patrick Marsh**

Cost: $9,000,000

2014				2015												2016							
Sept.	Oct.	Nov.	Dec.	Jan.	Feb.	Mar.	Apr.	May	Jun.	Jul.	Aug.	Sept.	Oct.	Nov.	Dec.	Jan.	Feb.	Mar.	Apr.	May	Jun.	Jul.

Patrick Marsh is the visionary behind the Creation Museum design and popular exhibits, which opened in 2007. He is now undertaking this mammoth project of overseeing the exhibits on the Ark Encounter.

I went to both the University of Southern California (USC) and University of California, Los Angeles (UCLA). I was very interested in architecture, graphic design, and three-dimensional things — sculpting; all of these were just sort of natural for me. However, once I was out of school, I was involved in the fashion business with a store in Beverly Hills, designing and producing high fashion women's clothing. I ended up doing that for ten years.

I went from that to work on the 1984 Summer Olympics in Los Angeles as a Production Designer for the Track and Field and Boxing Venues, in addition to the design of the backdrop for the Opening Ceremonies. From there, I worked as a Production Designer on the Statue of Liberty celebration in 1986. I was then hired as a Production Designer by Universal Studios, designing sets for the King Kong and Jaws attractions. I was there for three and a half years and learned a lot. The next ten years I was in Japan working on various theme parks and attractions including Puroland, the largest indoor theme park in Japan.

A Greater Vision

A friend told me about the Creation Museum being built in the Northern Kentucky area. My brother and his family lived in Indiana, and my wife and I used to come at Christmastime to stay with my family. During one Christmas visit, I met with Mike Zovath and Ken Ham, about designing the exhibits for the Creation Museum, and they hired me. I knew when I came back and met with Ken that all the things I had been learning my entire life would be a perfect fit to help with the Creation Museum. In reality, I was one of the few Christians that I knew of working in the theme park and attractions industry. I said to Ken, "If you write me a script, I would like to design something that makes the whole thing come alive." The rest is history, and since then almost three million people have been through the Creation Museum. This was the beginning of a long-term relationship between myself and Answers in Genesis. Now I am undertaking the project of a lifetime, the Ark Encounter.

With the Ark, there are multiple layers. First of all, we really wanted to create a biblical Ark — that was the priority, to make it out of wood so that it actually looked authentic. It would have the smell, feel, and the sound of a real wooden structure.

The purpose of the Ark is to be evangelistic, and we wanted it to be as realistic as we could make it. We also wanted to talk about all the aspects of what happened during the Flood, because the Flood is such an important event that everyone needs to know about and understand.

We really wanted to tell the story of how the Ark could be built, how big it was, what it looked like, and why. We were contacted by a guy named Tim Lovett who basically had been working on the concept for many years on his own. He is an engineer from Australia, and he had been working on developing the structure of the Ark — the physical concept of what it could look like, and how it functioned. He had studied ships, researched how to make the Ark seaworthy, and considered how Noah could have built it.

Also, John Woodmorappe wrote a book on what it would have been like if there were 16,000 animals on board the Ark; how much food, water, and air it would take, and all the necessities to be able to keep the people and animals alive. So you sort of pull all those pieces together and begin to design what the Ark could and would look like.

But the process all started with Ken — with the two of us deciding what we wanted to do and what we agreed upon, and then me putting together a master plan for everything that was going to be in the Ark and the reason why we were going to include it. For example, what the decks were all about and how they are going to be divided up to be able to tell the story. One by one, we gave information to the different designers of their specialty. Then the next process was to develop some scripts.

Where to Begin?

There is so much detail that is unknown in the biblical account, because God just basically came to Noah and said "Hey, the world has gone so crazy, and the people are so evil that I am going to get rid of them and start all over, and I want you to build a ship, and I want you to be able to take all of the animals that I will send you on board." The rest of it you have to make some assumptions about, such as who was Noah, how did he learn how to build all of this stuff, and what were his capabilities?

I started thinking through this whole thing and realized it only took us about 70 years in the U.S. to go from horse and buggy to placing a man on the moon. Since people in the time of Noah lived anywhere between 500 and 900 years of age, think of all the different things that they could have learned — what kind of abilities they had. The truth is, he could have accomplished a lot of things we will never know about because there was nothing left after the Flood.

We chose to divide the Ark into what I would call scientific exhibits, religious exhibits, and then Noahite exhibits. The first deck is basically filled with animals, so we've built cages that we believe could have worked for Noah and the animals. We show how these animals would have been cared for, fed, watered, and even cleaned up after.

Every exhibit starts with a premise. On the concept of, let's say, the blacksmith shop — we started looking at ancient tools and did as much historical research as possible. Same thing with the costumes. You figure out what people might have worn during that historical period, what the weather was like, what part of the country this was all in. We assume it was very much like the Middle East, but it also had a climate that was good for growing crops and all kinds of things.

So you start adding all of these pieces together, and you go, "Okay, I'm going to make a blacksmith shop. What are all the tools he could have used?" Then, we start looking at all the handmade tools that go into that. Then, wonder what kind of furnace he could have used, such as a bellows furnace, or something similar, to heat the materials. Then, you start developing ideas such as making tables out of wood and all the materials he might have, and you get a creative look and feel for what you need.

Next, we started working on the design concept and how we were

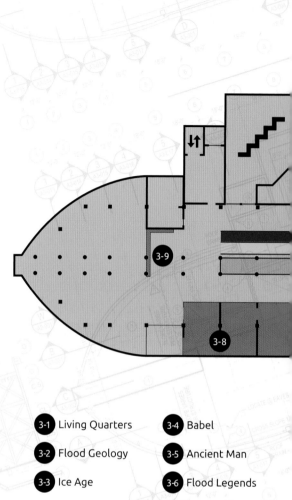

3-1 Living Quarters   3-4 Babel

3-2 Flood Geology   3-5 Ancient Man

3-3 Ice Age   3-6 Flood Legends

Deck 3 Exhibit Layout

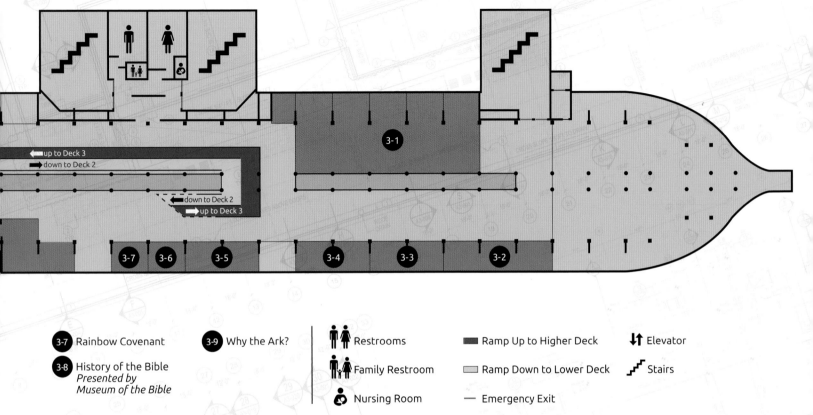

3-1

3-7   3-6   3-5   3-4   3-3   3-2

← up to Deck 3
→ down to Deck 2

← down to Deck 2
→ up to Deck 3

3-7 Rainbow Covenant

3-8 History of the Bible
*Presented by
Museum of the Bible*

3-9 Why the Ark?

Restrooms

Family Restroom

Nursing Room

Ramp Up to Higher Deck

Ramp Down to Lower Deck

— Emergency Exit

↕ Elevator

Stairs

Tools for Noah's workshop.

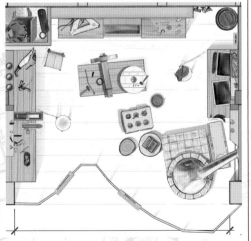

Blacksmith shop overview.

Pre-Flood world exhibit concept.

To the left you can see a detailed drawing of Shem's room.

Below, a drawing is marked with all the different items that will need to be made in order to bring this exhibit to a high-end finished state. There were over 40 items being designed, then given to the fabrication team to be created. Each has to be stained to have the look of antiquity for the Ark. A fashion team will design, sew, and colorize the linens for the desired look.

Here is a full-color drawing of Shem's room.

going to go about it. Is it going to be 3D or is it going to be two-dimensional like graphic design or illustration? Is it going to be a movie? Is it going to have sound effects?

First, we figure out what would be an interesting exhibit, and then, from there, we really start in earnest to do sketches. Next, we start figuring out how we are going to produce all of these things and the manpower needed to do it.

As the design process was continuing, we started making small mock-ups, models, and 3D paper models for all

the exhibits to see how they might turn out. This helps reveal what they would look like — doing color studies, renderings, all of those kinds of things. Then from there, once we got the okay on the scripts and models, we started playing around with some of the graphic ideas and explored what some of the color might look like. At this point, we started doing prototypes, little elements of different pieces to find the style and what it might be like. From the prototypes, we brought in some painters to do mock-ups in order to see how they would look before we got into actual production.

Here is a detailed blueprint for the fabrication team.

Noah's library finished and ready for the grand opening.

Shem's room completed.

Why It Matters

When a guest views an exhibit at the Ark Encounter are they (a) going to be pleased? and (b) going to get the message? Have we done it right? Are we telling the right narrative? We wouldn't be doing this if it weren't for the message. This entire place is only about the message. Everything beyond that is gloss. Outside of the Cross, we feel the Ark is the best example of salvation that there is. Noah and his family had to walk through the door of the Ark to be saved. You and I need to do the same, just as it says in John 10:9, "I am the door. If anyone enters by Me, he will be Saved…" That is the core message; that is why we are building the Ark. That is the truth we hope visitors will find.

You can't walk into the Ark without a sense of awe and "wow." There is a sense of godliness in the "awe factor," and I want to be sure that when people come here they will be impacted by what they see. We didn't just do this for ourselves; we want visitors to get a sense that "Wow, this is what Noah could have done. This is what the Ark could have looked like. This is what the Bible has to say. Wow, I had no idea it was this big, or it looked this way." My goal has really been to try to bring the Bible alive for people and to compromise as little as possible in the process if I can.

One thing I am most excited about is that each one of the exhibits has something incredibly special to focus on throughout the various aspects of the journey. I'm mechanically minded, so I really enjoy the exhibits that answer the question, "How did Noah do it?" I'm also a hands-on kind of guy, so I really like all of the exhibits that explain how these things work, and the science behind them is so incredible.

The structure of the Ark is very natural. You walk in and there is a smell to it; there is a sound to it, and when you walk up to a beam and you knock on it and discover it's not hollow. It's not fake. Everything else we do today is done in layers of fakeness. When we build a house, it's hollow. When we build a skyscraper, it's all this steel going up, and then you put a little façade of stone on the outside and glass; and in ten years, you can tear it down. It's gone. People are amazed when they visit Europe and other parts of the world where structures are made out of stone, made out of timber frame, and made just like the Ark. Made out of all these massive pieces of God's creation. There is something reverent about a piece of wood, a piece of stone, all of those kinds of things like mountains, things that are not something you just created out of your own intelligence.

There are two ways in which my life has prepared me for this moment. One is that God has been gracious and allowed me to have all these experiences and, as a result, I've learned an awful lot. I feel comfortable immersing myself in all these different kinds of creative things, because I've been through it in one way or another. Whether I've been directly involved with a film or whether I've just been a part of an experience — God has taken me through all of it. I understand it and know what a full production is like from beginning to end.

The second preparation is that I have opened quite a few theme parks, so it doesn't seem like such a scary thing anymore. I know what it is like to go through the last panic mode and still be able to open and work through it. There is no doubt God has prepared me the same way he prepared Noah to do what he had to do. It is incredible to me that God has taken me all over the world, to be able to see and do all the things that I've done; and then to come back to what I think of as rural Kentucky, and do what I think is the greatest thing I'll ever have the chance to do.

The Finished Product

	2014					2015												2016				
Aug.	Sept.	Oct.	Nov.	Dec.	Jan.	Feb.	Mar.	Apr.	May	Jun.	Jul.	Aug.	Sept.	Oct.	Nov.	Dec.	Jan.	Feb.	Mar.	Apr.	May	Jun.

Left: A section of the parking lot the first week of the Ark Encounter opening.

Below: The entrance road widened with the completed parking lot, striped and ready for the grand opening and the arrival of up to 4,000 cars.

The completed bow stands 104 feet off the ground.

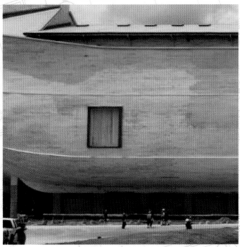

The door into the Ark on the second deck.

The completed stern with the blessing of a beautiful sunset.

ARK ENCOUNTER FACTS

Decking: 600,000 board-feet.

Plywood: 15,150 sheets of wood at 4 feet x 8 feet.

Bamboo flooring: 290,000 board-feet, which is around 55 miles of flooring.

Drilling: 67,467 holes drilled in the heavy timber, most were done by the CNC machine.

Steel plates: Steel plates and connections weighed in at 95 tons.

Wood pegs, bolts, washers and nuts: 50,000 used.

Total board-feet: 3.3 million board-feet of timber used for the Ark structure (not counting the wood in the exhibits). In board-feet, that would be 612 miles, the distance between Williamstown, Kentucky, and Philadelphia, Pennsylvania.

Heavy Timber: 5,435 pieces of timber were fabricated for this project.

Screws: There was a total of 300,000, anywhere from 3 inches to 24 inches long.

Concrete: 3,500 cubic yards of concrete will make a driveway that is 4 inches thick by 10 feet wide by 5.3 miles long.

Concrete blocks: Over 100,000 of the large size blocks: (16" x 8" x 12") were used in this project.

Pump: This pump was placed in a 50,000 gallon holding tank full of water for fire protection. It can pump 1,000 gallons a minute.

Harry, Craig, and Todd.

Acknowledgments

Todd Geer - *Vice President of Construction, Troyer Group*
Harry Morton - *Job Superintendent, Troyer Group*
Craig Baker – *President, First Companies (Answers in Genesis Board)*
There are a host of others that made this project possible as well:
Michael Zovath, LeRoy LaMontagne, Tim Schmitt, Doug Henderson, Jon Taylor, Kristen Andersen, Travis Wilson, Allen Greene, Harrison Craig, Chris Osborne, Orie and Ernest Lehman, and a cast of hundreds more.

Photo Credits:

Shannon Marie Hedlund, a Denver based photographer
Peter Kappes
Ken Ham
Tim Dudley
Maria Murphy
Colorado Timberframe, www.coloradotimberframe.com
Structural Wood Systems, www.structuralwood.com
Paul DeCesare

THINK
BIGGER

ARK
ENCOUNTER

Plan your visit at ArkEncounter.com

Williamstown, KY
(south of Cincinnati)